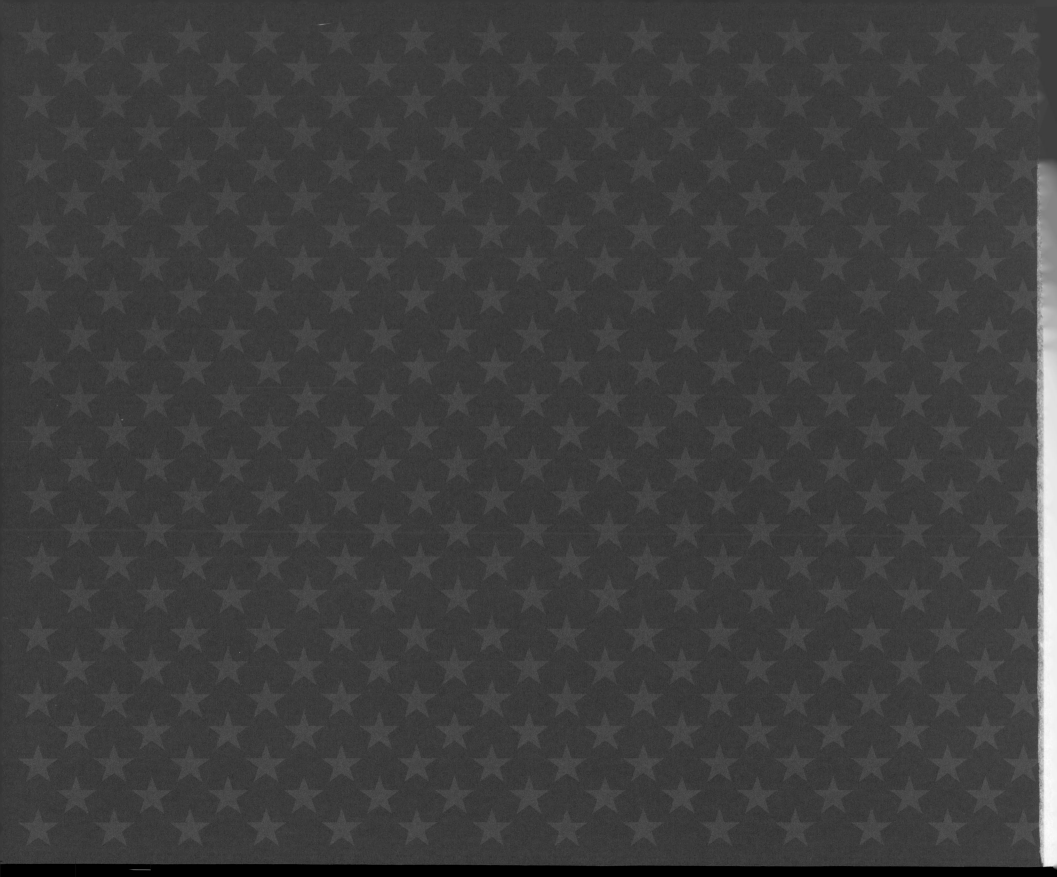

US MARINES
Alphabet Book

JERRY PALLOTTA ★ **SAMMIE GARNETT** ★ Illustrated by **VICKIE FRASER**

Charlesbridge

Thank you to Christopher Brighton, Billy Miller, Gregory Foos, and Michael Spencer—J. P.

Thank you to Randall Ricketts, Richard Clampitt, Matt Patmon, Gary Smith, Marisol Smith, Tommy Thomas, Virginia Thomas, and Benjamin Lee Tebault, a true American hero who gave his all for our country—S. G.

Thank you to all the Marine Corps public affairs officers who assisted in making this book possible—V. F.

The authors would like to thank USMC, the National USMC Museum, the USMC Heritage Foundation, Neil Abelsma, Loren Armas, Sona P. Babani, Ernest J. Barnes, Robert Blackman, Michael Blaha, Kelly Bridgewater, Jennifer Brofer, Jennifer Brown, David Burger, Bo Burwell, Bernie Campoli, Raymond Capers, Carlos R. Chavez, Ric Clampitt, Rob Cole, Arvil Cook, David Cram, Christina Delai, M. J. Delarosa, Jorge Dimmer, Brian Donnelley, Christopher Ebdon, AV8PIX.com, Kee Etsicitty, Jerry Flowers, Gregory Foos, Callie Fraser, Lee Fraswer, James R. Futreu, Bill Garnett, Robert B. Garrison, Bill Grein, Gary Harrell, Jacob Harrer, Dawn L. Harrison, James W. Heck, Bill Heiken, Bryan P. Howard, Daniel M. Huvane, Rebekah Ide, Victoria Jarvison, Yaphet K. Jones, Lena M. Kaljot, Tim Keefe, Brian Kester, C. Ray Kinney, Ben Kristy, Jeremy Lavine, Duane E. Lee, Dina Linn, Ashley Lira, Kyle Lira, Keith Little, Marty Lyman, Chris Lynch, Austin Mansfield, John Marion, Bill Mattocks, Kristen Merger, Jean Mildor, Scott Miller, Bill Moore, Yvonne Murphy, Chester Nez, Chanin Nuntavong, Nathan Odell, Tim Oliver, T. J. Oliver, Brian P. O'Rourke, Olivia Packenham, John J. Parry, Matt Patmon, Pete Poillon, Steven Ramus, Randall Ricketts, Rich Rodebaugh, Kristopher Russell, Barbara Schlatter, Philip Schulte, Jackie Scriven, Rick Scriven, Andy Sendry, B. J. Sevenson, Christopher Simms, Albert Smith, Gary Smith, Marisol Smith, Earl Speechley, Ryan Summers, Syndi Taite, Bill Toledo, Robert S. Torres, Samuel Tso, David Velez, Ken White, Brian Whittaker, Hank Winn, Stephen R. Wise, Woody Woodward, Haley Zelms, and Hunter Zelms.

Published by Charlesbridge
9 Galen Street, Watertown, MA 02472
(617) 926-0329 • www.charlesbridge.com

Library of Congress Cataloging-in-Publication Data
Names: Garnett, Sammie, author. | Pallotta, Jerry, author. | Fraser, Vickie, illustrator.
Title: US Marines alphabet book / Jerry Pallotta and Sammie Garnett; illustrated by Vickie Fraser.
Other titles: U.S. Marines alphabet book
Description: Watertown: Charlesbridge, [2021] | Audience: Ages 4–7 | Audience: Grades K–1 | Summary: "This alphabet book has something about the US Marines for every letter."—Provided by publisher.
Identifiers: LCCN 2020014302 (print) | LCCN 2020014303 (ebook) | ISBN 9781570919572 (hardcover) | ISBN 9781632897558 (ebook)
Subjects: LCSH: United States. Marine Corps—Juvenile literature. | Alphabet books—Juvenile literature. | English language—Alphabet—Juvenile literature.
Classification: LCC VE23 .G37 2021 (print) | LCC VE23 (ebook) | DDC 359.9/60973—dc23
LC record available at https://lccn.loc.gov/2020014302
LC ebook record available at https://lccn.loc.gov/2020014303

Printed in China
(hc) 10 9 8 7 6 5 4 3 2 1

Illustrations done in mixed media
Display type set in Rockwell by Monotype
Text type set in Memphis by Adobe Systems Inc.
Color separations and printing by 1010 Printing International Limited in Huizhou, Guangdong, China
Production supervision by Jennifer Most Delaney
Designed by Cathleen Schaad

Aa

A is for Assault Amphibious Vehicle.

When a navy ship reaches its destination, an assault amphibious vehicle, or AAV, transports marines from ship to shore. Then—surprise!—it can keep on going. This versatile vehicle operates on land as well as in the water. An AAV can travel four hundred miles inland before refueling. It can also travel fifty miles an hour on flat terrain.

Bb

B is for Bulldog. The official mascot of the US Marine Corps is a bulldog. Just like other marines, he wears a uniform and holds a military rank. He is named Chesty after the highly decorated marine general Lewis B. "Chesty" Puller. Chesty the bulldog is a celebrity at parades, dedications, and other special marine events.

Cc

C is for the Commandant's House. The commandant, a four-star general, is the highest-ranking officer in the US Marine Corps. This person lives in the Commandant's House, located on the oldest marine post in the country, the Marine Barracks in Washington, DC. The United States Marine Drum and Bugle Corps, known as "The Commandant's Own," performs at more than four hundred military and civilian events each year.

Dd

D is for Drill Instructor.
The drill instructor takes a nervous group of new recruits and trains the young men and women to be physically strong and mentally tough marines. Drill instructors instill a love of country, family, and the Marine Corps. And don't make fun of "the hat"!

Drill Instructor's Creed

"These recruits are entrusted to my care.

I will train them to the best of my ability.

I will develop them into smartly disciplined, physically fit, basically trained marines, thoroughly indoctrinated in love of corps and country.

I will demand of them, and demonstrate by my own example, the highest standards of personal conduct, morality, and professional skill."

E is for Emblem. The eagle, globe, and anchor make up the official emblem of the US Marine Corps. It was designed in 1868.

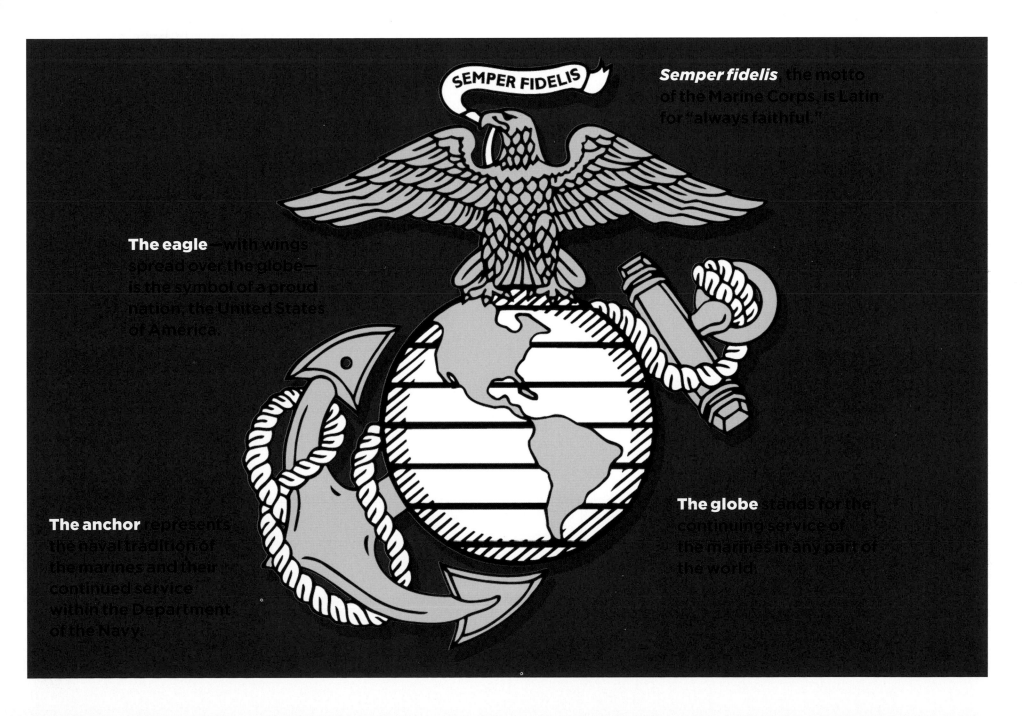

SEMPER FIDELIS

Semper fidelis, the motto of the Marine Corps, is Latin for "always faithful."

The eagle—with wings spread over the globe—is the symbol of a proud nation, the United States of America.

The anchor represents the naval tradition of the marines and their continued service within the Department of the Navy.

The globe stands for the continuing service of the marines in any part of the world.

Ff

F is for Fire Team. Four marines who work together in combat are called a fire team. All four are expert riflemen capable of quick and effective action in dangerous situations. Each member has a different responsibility. One is team leader, and the other members scout and carry extra ammunition and grenades. When a spoken command might reveal the team's location to an enemy, the leader gives orders silently, using hand and arm signals.

fire team

advance

go back

halt

G is for Guard Duty. Marine security guards protect diplomats, employees, and classified information at US embassies and consulates around the world. They also supervise visitors entering and exiting those embassies. If there is a riot, demonstration, or terrorist attack, marine security guards are trained to react.

MARINE CORPS EMBASSY SECURITY GROUP

"IN EVERY CLIME AND PLACE"

H is for Helicopter. Helicopters are rotary-wing aircraft that take off and land vertically. They have great nicknames: chopper, helo, whirlybird, and eggbeater. Can you think of another nickname for a helicopter? The marines use choppers to deliver troops, supplies, and heavy equipment.

Hh

USA 45

AH-1W SUPER COBRA

USA 53

CH-53D STALLION

Ii

I is for Inflatable Boats. Inflatable boats are used to transport marines onto beaches, piers, and larger vessels. These stealthy boats are seaworthy, lightweight, and easy to carry and store. They are perfect for ferrying sneaky reconnaissance teams to and from covert activities.

J is for Jet. A jet is a fixed-wing aircraft propelled by jet engines.

Wait a minute! What is this KC-130 doing on this page? It is not a jet. Can you guess why a KC-130 would be important to these jets?

KC-130 HERCULES

F/A-18 E/F HORNET

AV-8B HARRIER

E/A-6B PROWLER

The marines fly these jets:
- F/A-18A Hornet, a fighter attack jet
- AV-8B Harrier II, a jump jet that can take off and land vertically
- E/A-6B Prowler, an electronic-warfare jet

K is for KA-BAR. A KA-BAR knife is a fighting knife used in hand-to-hand combat. The marines discovered that the KA-BAR knife could also be used to open ration cans, dig foxholes, pound tent stakes, drive nails, and cut roots and wood. It's a multipurpose tool!

L is for Leatherneck. The nickname "leatherneck" does not refer to marines' well-known toughness. The name comes from the leather collar on early marine uniforms. The leather collar was replaced by the smart-looking standing collar worn today. The marines have many other nicknames, including jarhead, devil dog, soldier of the sea, and gyrene.

Mm

M is for Marine Band. These marines carry musical instruments instead of rifles. The wonderful musicians of the United States Marine Band inspire patriotism whenever they perform. President Thomas Jefferson called the marine band "The President's Own" when it played at his inauguration in 1801. Composer John Philip Sousa is the most famous member of the marine band and served as its director from 1880 to 1892.

John Philip Sousa, "The March King"

"THE PRESIDENT'S OWN"
UNITED STATES MARINE BAND

N is for Navajo Code Talkers. In the early months of World War II, when the US armed forces discovered that their secret messages were being intercepted by the enemy, Navajo Code Talkers came to the rescue. Twenty-nine young Navajo marines developed an unbreakable code by combining their native language with military vocabulary. The Navajo code gave American troops an advantage, saved thousands of lives, and helped win the war. (See the Navajo Code Talker Alphabet on page 31.)

Nn

Oo

O is for Osprey. What would happen if you combined a helicopter with an airplane? The result would be an MV-22 Osprey, a revolutionary hybrid design with rotors that tilt. Not only can it fly as fast and as far as an airplane, carry twenty-four fully loaded combat marines, and refuel in midair, it can also take off and land vertically in almost any terrain.

Pp

P is for Parris Island. For recruits from east of the Mississippi River, thirteen weeks of training start at the recruit depot on Parris Island, South Carolina. The future marines go through rigorous mental and physical training while learning the values of the Marine Corps. Recruit training ends with the Crucible, a fifty-four-hour exercise that calls for the highest level of teamwork, determination, and discipline. During this exercise, the recruits march forty-eight miles carrying a forty-five-pound pack and rifle, and they complete twenty-nine complex problem-solving tasks, all with very little food or sleep.

Recruits from west of the Mississippi River report to the recruit depot in San Diego, California, for their training.

Qq

Q is for Quantico. Marine Corps Base Quantico is known as the crossroads of the US Marine Corps. It has become the hub of marine training, education, and technology. The principles, policies, and practices of the marines are developed here. Quantico is also home to the beautiful National Museum of the Marine Corps.

Rr

R is for Reserves. Men and women in the Marine Corps Reserve are trained marines who live and work in your community. Along with marines on active duty, members of the Marine Corps Reserve are prepared and ready for action in case of war or a national emergency. Your neighbor, school principal, firefighter, nurse, or baseball coach might serve as a marine reservist.

Ss

S is for Sword. Although marines no longer use swords as weapons, swords are worn at parades and special events. When marines marry, they have the option of wearing their dress uniform. The bride and groom often use the sword to cut the wedding cake. Officers wear a Mameluke sword, shown on the left, and noncommissioned officers wear the marine noncommissioned officer sword, shown on the right.

Tt

T is for Toys for Tots. The Toys for Tots program was started in 1947 by a marine reservist. The purpose of the program is to collect donated toys and distribute them to needy children during the holiday season. The very first toy donated was a Raggedy Ann–style doll. Walt Disney designed the Toys for Tots logo and the program's first poster. Toys for Tots is an official activity of the US Marine Corps and an official mission of the Marine Corps Reserve.

Uu

U is for Uniforms. It is easy to tell officers from enlisted marines. Their uniforms are different. Marines wear work uniforms, combat uniforms, and dress uniforms, and the uniforms change with the seasons and the weather.

Marines are known for always looking sharp. Marine "dress blues" have all three colors of the American flag—red, white, and blue.

Vv

V is for Veteran. A veteran is any person who has served as a member of the US armed forces. These patriotic individuals who love and support our country can be found all over the United States. Let's give a big thank-you to all veterans who put themselves in harm's way to defend our nation. Cheer them on at the next Veterans Day, Fourth of July, or Memorial Day parade.

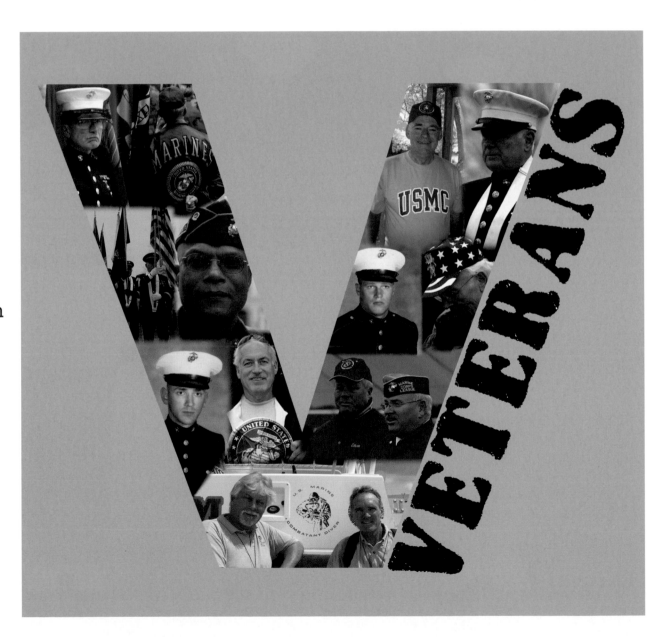

W is for Weapon. Marines carry a variety of weapons. They may be armed with a rifle or a combat knife. A marine is armed with other weapons as well: diligent training, mental toughness, love of country, and the desire to serve.

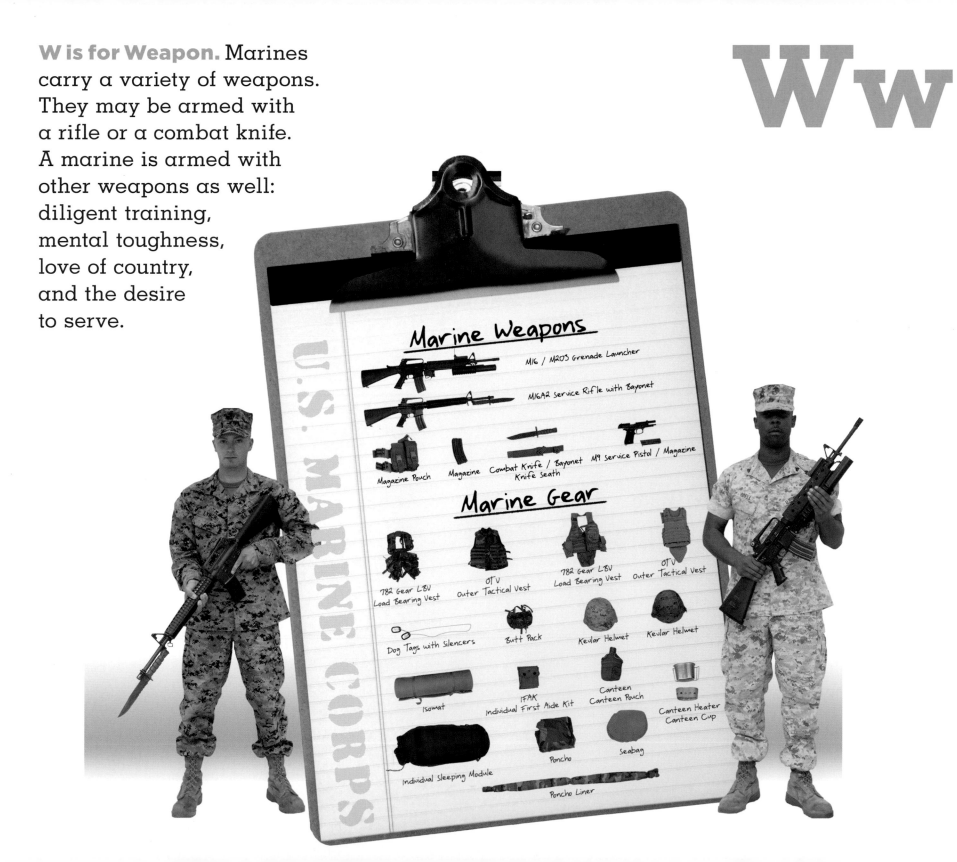

Ww

U.S. MARINE CORPS

Marine Weapons

- M16 / M203 Grenade Launcher
- M16A2 Service Rifle with Bayonet
- Magazine Pouch
- Magazine
- Combat Knife / Bayonet Knife Seath
- M9 Service Pistol / Magazine

Marine Gear

- 782 Gear LBV Load Bearing Vest
- OTV Outer Tactical Vest
- 782 Gear LBV Load Bearing Vest
- OTV Outer Tactical Vest
- Dog Tags with Silencers
- Butt Pack
- Kevlar Helmet
- Kevlar Helmet
- Isomat
- IFAK Individual First Aide Kit
- Canteen Canteen Pouch
- Canteen Heater Canteen Cup
- Individual Sleeping Module
- Poncho
- Seabag
- Poncho Liner

Xx

X is for HMX-1. Marine Helicopter Squadron One, or HMX-1, provides transportation for the president of the United States. "Marine One" is the helicopter's call sign when the president is on board. It is common for it to land on the South Lawn at the White House. From there, it is a fast ride to Andrews Air Force Base or Camp David. The HMX-1 helicopters used to transport the president and other important people are called white tops.

Y is for Yellow Footprints. "Get off my bus! Stand on the yellow footprints, NOW!" yells a marine drill instructor. Yellow footprints show recruits at basic training how to stand in military formation. The fun of becoming a US marine has just begun!

After recruit graduation, many marines return to the yellow footprints to share their arrival experience with family and friends.

Yy

Zz

Z is for Zero In. Every marine who completes recruit training is a skilled rifleman. Marines are often the first to arrive in a battle zone—accurate marksmanship is important! Imagine looking through the sights of a rifle. Through practice, practice, and more practice on the rifle range, marines learn to zero in on targets and hit the bull's-eye.

NAVAJO CODE TALKER ALPHABET

(a parital list)

Alphabet	Navajo Word	English Word
A	wol-la-chee	ant
B	shush	bear
C	moasi	cat
D	be	deer
E	dzeh	elk
F	ma-e	fox
G	klizzie	goat
H	lin	horse
I	tkin	ice
J	ah-ya-tsinne	jaw
K	klizzie-yazzie	kid
L	dibeh-yazzie	lamb
M	na-as-tso-si	mouse
N	a-chin	nose
O	ne-ahs-jah	owl
P	bi-so-dih	pig
Q	ca-yeilth	quiver
R	gah	rabbit
S	dibeh	sheep
T	than-zie	turkey
U	no-da-ih	Ute
V	a-keh-di-glini	victor
W	gloe-ih	weasel
X	al-na-as-dzoh	cross
Y	tsah-as-zih	yucca
Z	besh-do-tliz	zinc

HONOR
COURAGE
COMMITMENT

SEMPER FIDELIS

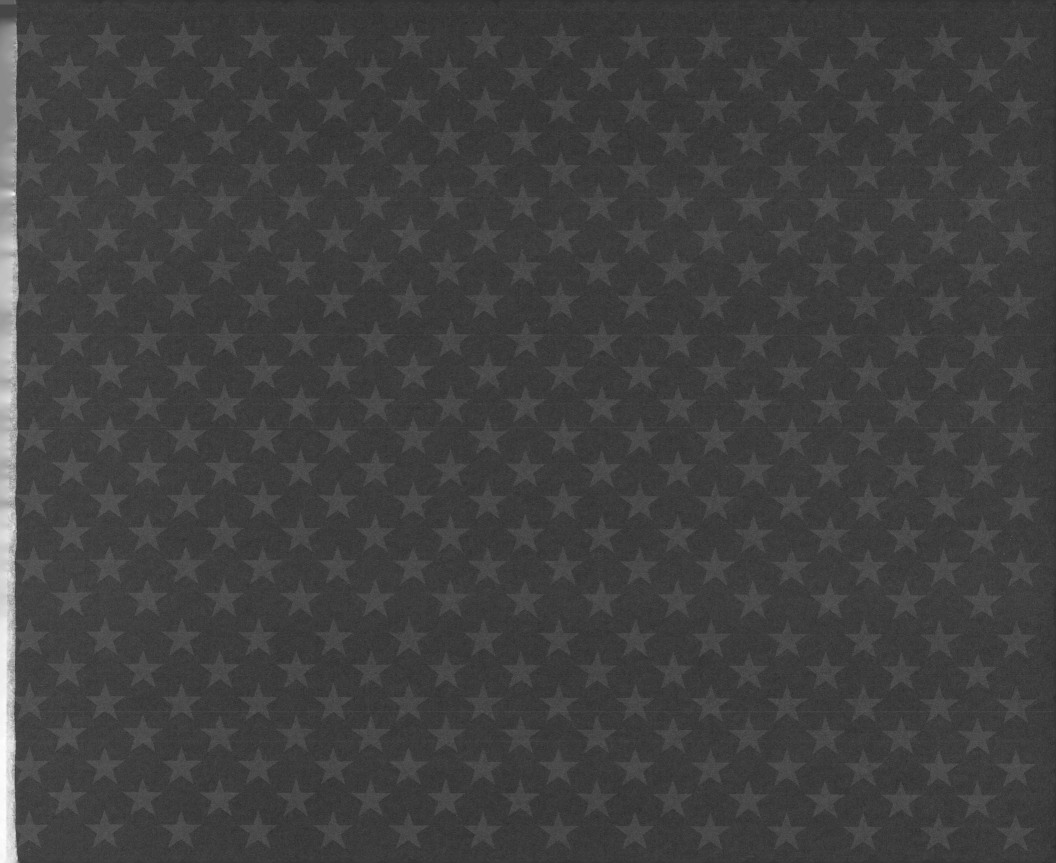